THE LEOPARD SON

A True Story

Words by Jackie Ball and Kit Carlson

DISCOVERY
CHANNEL
BOOKS™

LEARNING
TRIANGLE
PRESS

*Connecting
kids, parents, and teachers
through learning*

An imprint of McGraw-Hill

New York San Francisco Washington, D.C. Auckland Bogotá Caracas
Lisbon London Madrid Mexico City Milan Montreal New Delhi
San Juan Singapore Sydney Tokyo Toronto

McGraw-Hill

A Division of The **McGraw·Hill** Companies

Copyright © 1996 by the Discovery Channel.
Published by Learning Triangle Press, an imprint of McGraw-Hill.

This book is printed on acid-free paper.

hb   1 2 3 4 5 6 7 8 9 DOW/DOW 9 0 0 9 8 7 6

McGraw-Hill books are available at special quantity discounts to use as premiums and sales promotions, or for use in corporate training programs. For more information, please write to the Director of Special Sales, McGraw-Hill, 11 West 19th Street, New York, NY 10011. Or contact your local bookstore.

Library of Congress Cataloging-in-Publication Data

Discovery Channel (Firm)
The leopard son / by The Discovery Channel.
p. cm.
Summary: Describes the leopards of Tanzania and their interaction with the other animals there.
ISBN 0-07-016061-9 (hc)
1. Leopard--Tanzania--Serengeti Plain--Juvenile literature.
[1. Leopard. 2. Zoology--Tanzania.] I. Title.
QL737.C23D48 1996
599.74'428--DC20   96-28048
                                        CIP
                                          AC

Acquisitions: Judith Terrill-Breuer, Editor-in-Chief
Editors: Ellen Foley James; Judith Terrill-Breuer
Design: David Whitmore
Photography Editor: Ede Rothaus

Photo credits: Karl & Kathy Amman/Bruce Coleman, Inc. (13); Sean Avery/Planet Earth Pictures (2 bottom); Anthony Bannister (16); Ofer Bahat (23 top); Tom Brakefield/BCI (15); Erwin & Peggy Bauer/Bruce Coleman, Inc. (11 bottom, 25); C&M Denis-Huot/Peter Arnold, Inc. (20/21); Wolfgang Kaehler (8 center); Hugo van Lawick (3, 7 bottom, 30); The Leopard Son film—Hugo van Lawick, Matthew Aeberhard Cinematographers (2 center, 7 top; 8 top, 9 top, 9 center, 18 top, 18 bottom; 21; 24; 26 bottom); Peter Lillie/A.B.P.L. (26/27); David Madison (16 top); Luiz Claudio Marigo/Peter Arnold, Inc. (2 top); Mark Newman (11 top); Boyd Norton (19); Fritz Pölking/Dembinsky Photo Association (14, 28); Jonathan Scott/Planet Earth Pictures (8/9, 12 top; 23 bottom); Anup Shah/Planet Earth Pictures (1, 6, 10/11, 17 bottom, 26 top); Art Wolfe (17 top; 22, 29)

THE LEOPARD SON

A True Story

The Tree

In the highlands of East Africa, there is a vast plain. The tribal people who live here call it "the wide place," or Serengeti. And it is *so* vast, and *so* wide, that millions of animals roam about freely.

Huge herds of curly-horned wildebeests dot the plain. Baby elephants shuffle alongside their mothers, trunks swaying. Galloping zebras stop suddenly to graze under an acacia tree.

At the very top of this umbrella-shaped tree, in a nest made of sticks, a hungry snake eagle chick waits for its mother to bring back breakfast. A giraffe moves around the edges of the tree, sniffing and poking its long, black tongue high into the branches for a mouthful of delicate leaves.

On a lower branch, another animal waits for food. It is a leopard cub, just two months old. He scrapes his tiny claws against the rough bark. He yawns. With one fat, furry paw, he swipes at a fly buzzing around his nose. Then he curls up, snug in the crook of his tree. When his mother is away, all he can do is wait.

Every few days, his mother goes out onto the wide plain to hunt for food. Since leopards live alone, there is no other animal to guard her son. So she hides him high up in their acacia tree home.

The Danger

But even the tree is not completely safe. The plain below is alive with danger, with animals who hunt and kill for their meals. They also have babies to feed, and if those babies are to grow up, they too must eat.

The leopard son raises his head. He is small, but his senses are as sharp as a knife. Something is approaching. His ears swivel like periscopes, listening, listening. His nose twitches as if it were alive, sniffing, sniffing.

Below, a pair of green eyes stares up at him through the acacia's branches. For a moment, the cub is not afraid, just curious. He is too young to know that the lion is his enemy.

The creature roars—a sound like distant thunder. From neck to tail, the cub's fur rises, and he scrambles as far along the branch as he can go. Balancing

on the thinnest twigs, swaying in the wind, he is trapped. The lion begins to climb toward him. But just in time, a family of elephants lumbers past, their heavy steps shaking the tree. Startled, the lion bounds away into the tall, golden grass.

The Rescue

The cub dives into a dark hole in the tree to hide. But the lion's roar has given away his secret hiding place, and a spotted hyena follows the sound, to see what the lion has found.

Peeking out, the cub can see the hyena's blunt, black snout, the large ears, the enormous teeth. A strange whooping noise comes from its throat, each cry rising like a siren.

Then suddenly, the mother leopard is home. She dashes to the rescue, lunging and swiping at the hyena with her razor-sharp claws. The hyena backs off, scuttling sideways until he is out of sight.

As his mother leaps into the acacia tree, the cub scrambles toward her. He nuzzles and bites her nose. He rubs against her as if he can't get close enough, swishing his pointy tail across her face like a furry windshield wiper. At last he settles down at her side, and she licks him clean with her rough, pink tongue, smoothing his ruffled fur and soothing his fear.

The Lesson

But the peaceful moment can't last. The leopard mother must teach her son the lessons of life: how to hunt, how to hide, how to tell when danger is near. Carefully, she slinks down a branch to the ground, looking right and left for enemies. Slipping and sliding, head over heels, the cub tumbles down the trunk after her.

Bump! He hits the ground with a thud. When he looks up, his mother is gone. Only the white underside of her tail shows above the grass, waving like a banner at the head of a parade. With short, bounding leaps, he follows.

Even his mother becomes a toy. He sees her resting in the grass, her long, slender tail twitching slightly. He launches himself at the fluffy white rope, wrestling it, wrapping it around his neck, gnawing at it with squeals of delight. His mother lies there patiently, giving him only an occasional cuff on the ears or a light bite on the neck.

She lets him play, for, like all young animals, he plays for a purpose. This is how the cub will learn the skills he needs to stay alive.

The Seasons

On the Serengeti, there are only two seasons: wet and dry. In the dry season, the grassy plain becomes a desert. The plants and shrubs wither and die. Then the gazelles and wildebeests and zebras move on, heading for places where rain falls and the grass is green.

For the animals who stay, food is scarce, and hunting for a meal can take a very long time. As her son grows, the leopard mother has to travel even farther from home to find enough food for both of them.

Even though he is bigger now, the leopard son is still a cub—and for him, life is still a game. A leaf floating to the ground becomes a ball on an invisible string, to be smacked and swatted until it lies in tatters.

A towering termite mound is a sandcastle, ready to topple. Turtles are big mudpies to pat, then to stuff into his mouth.

It is getting hotter and drier. There has been no rain for weeks. While his mother is gone, the cub lolls on a shady branch, panting to keep cool. Above him, the mother snake eagle protects her chick from the sun by spreading her wings like an umbrella over the nest.

The Playmate

Nearby, something rustles the branches. It is a giraffe, looking for lunch. The cub slinks down the tree to sneak up on the spindly legs from behind. Not even as tall as the giraffe's knees,

he can only pounce around the ankles of the beast, teasing it until it dances away to the other side of the tree.

But the cub still wants to play. He climbs back up into the acacia, then

totters down a thin branch. As the giraffe snakes out its tongue and wiggles its lips, the young leopard bats at its face. Surprised, the giraffe blinks and bounces away. Finally he lopes off, looking for a quieter picnic spot.

The Chick

Early one morning, while the sun is still low in the sky, the mother snake eagle flies off to find food. The leopard son is waiting for his own mother to come home. He hangs like a gymnast on a bar, chin and front paws propped on a branch, his eyes half-closed.

A small sound awakens him—hardly a noise at all, just a very faint cheeping at the top of his tree. He has heard it before, but this time it seems to be calling to him. He climbs slowly up the narrow branches and peers into the big nest of tangled gray sticks. Terrified, the snake eagle chick stares back at him with round, yellow eyes.

Bouncing on the fragile branches, the cub prods the nest with one large paw. He sees his own wide shadow looming over the small creature. He lifts his nose to the hot, dry wind for a sign of change in the air. Turning his ears this way and that, he hears only the sound of leaves rustling below.

The young leopard does not hurt the little bird who shares his home; he just looks and sniffs and listens. Then he climbs back down the tree to his branch to wait for his mother.

The Flight

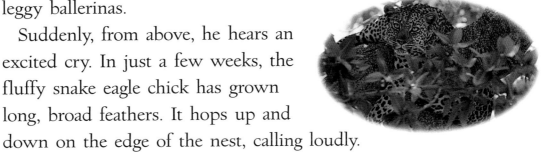

One day, the mother leopard heads out onto the plain, away from the acacia tree and her son. She has left him a big meal—a plump gazelle, which he helped her carry into the tree.

All alone, the leopard son waits, lounging on a branch, listening for the sound of his mother's soft steps in the grass. Down on the plain, ostriches flap up clouds of dust, their feathers fluffed out like tutus on leggy ballerinas.

Suddenly, from above, he hears an excited cry. In just a few weeks, the fluffy snake eagle chick has grown long, broad feathers. It hops up and down on the edge of the nest, calling loudly. Overhead, its mother soars in circles, watching her young one struggle to fly.

Then, in a rush, the young eagle flaps around the nest a couple of times, wobbles to the edge, and hops off into space. It flies—unsteadily at first, but soon it is gliding and swooping like a proud miniature of its majestic mother. The snake eagle has found its wings!

The Wait

While he waits for his mother, the leopard son gets hungrier and hungrier, hotter and hotter. The Serengeti looks like a sea of yellow straw, and the dry stalks crackle under his paws when he climbs down to prowl around the base of his tree. It still has not rained. The acacia has lost all its blossoms, and the giraffes and gazelles no longer come to nibble at its branches. The snake eagle chick has flown away. The leopard son waits, but there is no sign of his mother's tail coming toward him, waving at him above the tall grass. She has moved away to another tree so that he can finish his growing up. Now that he is old enough to hunt for himself, he no longer needs her, because her lessons have taught him well.

One morning, the leopard wakes to the steady splatter of rain on his fur. The long, dry season is over at last. The waterholes fill with rain. Elephants gather, slurping up the cool water with their trunks and spraying themselves. Cheetah cubs romp and tumble through puddles, turning into tiny bundles of spiky, wet fur. Giraffes glide through the damp dust, heads swaying in the sudden shower. The world is washed clean.

The Hunter

The leopard son bends over a pool to lap up the fresh rain. The water's surface is like a mirror, and the animal he sees there is very different from the tiny cub who once cowered at a lion's roar. He is big now. His light-and-dark spotted fur looks so much like scattered shadows that he is almost invisible in the thick grass. His enormous teeth and claws are deadly weapons for hunting or fighting. And he has the speed and strength to chase and catch swift, large animals.

He raises his head and sniffs the air. He is hungry. If he wants to eat, he will have to set out on his own. It is time to leave the acacia tree.

He stalks away from the pool, looking right and left for enemies, as his mother taught him. From somewhere nearby a lion roars, but the leopard son does not run from the sound. With a swish of his tail, he disappears into the tall grass. He will make his own way now on the wide Serengeti.

The Filmmaker

Hugo van Lawick

As a child growing up in Indonesia, England, and Holland, my dream was to work with animals and be a part of the great outdoors. I consider myself very lucky to have spent more than thirty-five years studying and documenting the wildlife of East Africa. Living in tented camps and rising before dawn each morning, I spend almost every day observing and filming some of nature's greatest dramas. More than a place to work, this has become my home.

In my mind, there is no place more magical than Africa's Serengeti—"the wide place," as it is called by the Maasai tribe. And there is no character more intriguing than the elusive leopard. For more than two years, I followed the coming-of-age of one young cub. With my camera, I watched as he learned, through play, the important skills of survival and hunting from his mother. Through my lens I shared tender, humorous, unpredictable, and sometimes frightening challenges of his growing up. I traveled many miles with him as a young adult, as he explored the world beyond his mother's territory. I followed him back again too, and became witness to the surprising turns in his life's story.

My childhood hopes have come true in Africa's wilderness, one of the last great wild places on earth. To be able to share its wonder with children brings my lifetime pursuit full circle.

Hugo van Lawick